GW00832117

Research Design in Social Science

By

Dr. V.K. Hamza

Published by:
VK Hamza
Copyright © 2000 - 2014, CreateSpace, a DBA of On-Demand Publishing, LLC.
www.amazon.com
Online purchase of the Book through
https://www.createspace.com/4798403

ISBN-13: 978-1523485567
ISBN-10: 1523485566
BISAC: Social Science / Research

No Part of this book may be reproduced or transmitted in any for or by any means, electronic or mechanical including photocopying, recording or by any transformation storage and retrieval system without written permission from the Author/Publisher

Indemnification Clause: This book is being sold/distributed subject to the exclusive condition that neither the author nor the publishers, individually or collectively, shall be responsible to indemnify the buyer/user/possessor of this book beyond the selling price of this book for any reason under any circumstances. If you do not agree to it, please do not buy/accept/use/possess this book

In Loving Memory of
My Revered Father and Mother
(The Fountain of Inspiration)

Acknowledgement

I will always remain grateful to God for his abundant blessings during the preparation of this book. This book consists of a critical evaluation of various social science research designs usually followed by the researchers during their dissertation. Through this book, a reader can get the idea of various research designs in the field of social science disciplines. This book is more useful to such students who are conducting studies as part of their academic as well as professional purposes. I have to thank several people including my parents, teachers, family, friends, and colleagues as they extended full support for designing the second edition of the book.

V.K. Hamza

Preface

This book has designed for catering the needs of students and scholars in the field of social science research study. Each design in the social science research have been discussed in detail that helps the reader to understand deeply the suitability of every such design. I forward this book to all students, researcher, teachers and everyone who interested to know the social science research designs available for conducting a new research independently.

Content

1. Introduction

A research design is the framework or plan for a study used as a guide in collecting and analyzing data. It gives a detailed outline of how an investigation will take place. A research design will typically include how data is to be collected, what instruments will be employed, how the instruments will be used and the intended means for analyzing data collected.

2. Need for Research Design

Research design is needed because it facilitates the smooth sailing of the various research operations, thereby making research as efficient as possible yielding maximal information with minimal expenditure of effort, time and money. Research design has a significant impact on the reliability of the results obtained. It thus acts as a firm foundation for the entire research. Following are the benefits to the researcher for having a good research design.

1

- It reduces inaccuracy;
- Helps to get maximum efficiency and reliability;
- Eliminates bias and marginal errors;
- Minimizes wastage of time;
- Helpful for collecting research materials;
- Helpful for testing of hypothesis;
- Gives an idea regarding the type of resources required in terms of money, manpower, time, and efforts;
- Provides an overview to other experts;
- Guides the research in the right direction
- Consumes less time.
- Ensures project time schedule.
- Helps researcher to prepare himself to carry out research in a proper and a systematic way.
- Better documentation of the various activities while the project work is going on.
- Helps in proper planning of the resources and their procurement in right time.
- Provides satisfaction and confidence, accompanied with a sense of success from the beginning of the work of the research project.

3. Types of Research Design

There are three basic types of research design: exploratory, descriptive, and causal. The names of the three types of research design describe their purpose very well. The goal of exploratory research is to discover ideas and in-sights. Descriptive research is usually concerned with describing a population with respect to important variables. Causal research is used to establish cause-and-effect relationships between variables. Experiments are commonly used in causal research designs because they are best suited to determine cause and effect.

4. Exploratory Research Design

Exploratory research is conducted to provide a better understanding of a situation. It isn't designed to come up with final answers or decisions. Through exploratory research, researchers hope to produce hypotheses about what is going on in a situation. It becomes the base for further study as it explores the reason or trend in the past. For e.g. as a researcher you might use exploratory research to provide insights about what caused the decrease in revenue. Suppose that you conducted interviews with potential car buyers and noticed that they seemed to be more excited about the new styles of other car brands than they were about the brand in question. This might lead to the hypothesis that style preferences had changed, resulting in lower sales. You can't really confirm or reject the hypothesis with exploratory research, though. That job is left for descriptive and/or causal research (quantitative research).

Exploratory research (sometimes referred to as qualitative research) shouldn't be expected to provide answers to the decision problem that the researcher attempting to solve through a study. It can provide very rich, meaningful information or even definitive explanations for particular individuals but exploratory research doesn't provide definitive answers for the overall population. There are two reasons for this such as exploratory research usually involves only a relatively small group of people, and these people are almost never randomly selected to participate.

There are often several possible hypotheses about a given marketing phenomenon, and exploratory research help to identify which research problem(s) ought to be pursued. It is also used to increase a researcher's familiarity with a problem, especially when the researcher doesn't know much about the organization and/or problem to be studied.

4.1. Types of Exploratory Research Designs

Through exploratory research, the researcher develops the familiarity with basic details, setting and concern. It provides a well grounded picture of the situation being developed or investigated. Through this the researcher can determine whether the study is feasible or refine the issue more systematically for investigation. In order to generate new ideas and tentative theories, the researcher usually conducts the following types of exploratory research designs

4.1.1. Literature Review

When the investigator proceeds on the path of research he has to take advantage of his predecessors. This technique will save time, cash, and effort. One of the quickest and least costly ways to discover hypotheses is to conduct a literature search. Almost all marketing research projects should start here. There is an incredible amount of information available in libraries, through online sources, in commercial data bases, and so on. The literature search may involve popular press (newspapers, magazines, etc.), trade literature, academic literature, or published statistics from research firms or governmental agencies. Review and perusal of pertinent literature is very helpful for researcher. Apart from literature directly related to the problem in hand, the literature that is related to similar problems is also very useful. It helps in the formulation of the problem

4.1.2. Experience Survey/Depth Interview

Some people are great source of information. It is better to interview those individuals who know about the subject. The objectives of such survey are to obtain insight into the relationship between variables and new ideas relating to the research problem. Anyone with relevant information is a potential candidate for a depth interview or experience survey, including current customers, members of the target market, executives and managers of the client organization, sales representatives, wholesalers, retailers, and so on.

The respondents picked are interviewed by the researcher. The researcher should prepare an interview schedule for the systematic questioning of informants. Thus an experience survey may enable the researcher to define the problem more consciously and help in the formulation of hypothesis. This survey may as well also offer information about the practical possibilities for doing different types of research. A number of interviews can be very costly. Well-trained interviewers demand high salaries; data are gathered from one respondent at a time; and, if recorded, audio/video recordings should be transcribed, coded, and examined. This method, however, can deliver important insights and more often than not is well worth the effort.

4.1.3. Focus Groups

Focus group interviews are among the most often used techniques in marketing research. Some would argue that they are among the most overused and misused techniques as well. In a focus group, a small number of individuals (e.g., 8–12) are brought together to talk about some topic of interest to the focus group sponsor. The discussion is directed by a moderator who is in the room with the focus group participants; managers, ad agency representatives, and/or others often watch the session from outside the room via a two-way mirror or video link. The moderator attempts to follow a rough outline of issues while simultaneously having the comments made by each person considered in group discussion. Participants are thus exposed to the ideas of others and can respond to those ideas with their own. The majority of the organizations engaging in the focus groups first screen the candidates to find out who will compose the particular group. Organizations also make sure to avoid groups, in which some of the participants have their relatives and friends, as this result in a one-sided discussion.

Group interaction is the key aspect that distinguishes focus group interviews from depth interviews, which are conducted with one respondent at a time. It is also the primary advantage of the focus group over most other exploratory techniques. Because of their interactive nature, ideas sometimes drop "out of the blue" during a focus group discussion. In addition, there is a snowballing effect: A comment by one individual can trigger a chain of responses from others. As a result, responses are often more spontaneous and less conventional than they might be in a depth interview.

4.1.3.1. The Role of Moderator.

The moderator in the focus group plays the single most important and most difficult role in the process. For instance, the moderator typically translates the study objectives into a guidebook. The moderator's guide book lists the general (and specific) issues to be addressed during the session, placing them in the general order in which the topics should arise. In general, a funnel approach is used; with broad general topics first and then increasing focus on the specific issues to be studied. As the moderator, researcher must understand the background of the problem and what the client needs to learn from the research process. Without this information, it's impossible to develop the guidebook and conduct a focus group effectively.

In general, moderator should be "flexible, objective, empathic, persuasive, and a good listener". In an ideal focus group, the moderator would just participate to put research topics. It is participants who must dominate the discussion. However, there are a number of situations where moderator should also participate. In order to prevent single participants or small groups from dominating the discussion and encourage reserved members to become involved, to reflat the discussion using provocative questions and for steering the discussion toward a deepening, the moderator may involve in the discussion.

4.1.4. Case Study

Case studies emphasize detailed contextual analysis of a limited number of events or conditions and their relationships. Researchers have used the case study research method for many years across a variety of disciplines. Social scientists, in particular, have made wide use of this qualitative research method to examine contemporary real-life situations and provide the basis for the application of ideas and extension of methods. Researcher has to examine existing records, observe the phenomenon as it occurs, conduct unstructured interviews, or use any one of a variety of other approaches to analyze what is happening in a given situation.

Critics of the case study method believe that the study of a small number of cases can offer no grounds for establishing reliability or generality of findings. Others feel that the intense exposure to study of the case biases the findings. Some dismiss case study research as useful only as an exploratory tool. Yet researchers continue to use the case study research method with success in carefully planned and crafted studies of real-life situations, issues, and problems.

Case analyses can be performed in lots of different ways. Sometimes internal records are reviewed, sometimes individuals are interviewed, and sometimes situations or people are observed carefully. A step by step approach for conducting case study is mentioned below

Step 1. Determine and Define the Research Questions

The first step in case study research is to establish a firm research focus to which the researcher can refer over the course of study of a complex phenomenon or object. The researcher establishes the focus of the study by forming questions about the situation or problem to be studied and determining a purpose for the study. The research object in a case study is often a program, an entity, a person, or a group of people. Each object is likely to be intricately connected to political, social, historical, and personal issues, providing wide ranging possibilities for questions and adding complexity to the case study. The researcher investigates the object of the case study in depth using a variety of data gathering methods to produce evidence that leads to understanding of the case and answers the research questions.

Case study research generally answers one or more questions which begin with "how" or "why." The questions are targeted to a limited number of events or conditions and their inter-relationships. To assist in targeting and formulating the questions, researchers conduct a literature review. This review establishes what research has been previously conducted and leads to refined, insightful questions about the problem. Careful definition of the questions at the start pinpoints where to look for evidence and helps determine the methods of analysis to be used in the study. The literature review, definition of the purpose of the case study, and early determination of the potential audience for the final report guide how the study will be designed, conducted, and publicly reported.

Step 2. Select the Cases and Determine Data Gathering and Analysis Techniques

During the design phase of case study research, the researcher determines what approaches to use in selecting single or multiple real-life cases to examine in depth and which instruments and data gathering approaches to use. When using multiple cases, each case is treated as a single case. Each case's conclusions can then be used as information contributing to the whole study, but each case remains a single case. Exemplary case studies carefully select cases and carefully examine the choices available from among many research tools available in order to increase the validity of the study. Careful discrimination at the point of selection also helps erect boundaries around the case.

The researcher must determine whether to study cases which are unique in some way or cases which are considered typical and may also select cases to represent a variety of geographic regions, a variety of size parameters, or other parameters. A useful step in the selection process is to repeatedly refer back to the purpose of the study in order to focus attention on where to look for cases and evidence that will satisfy the purpose of the study and answer the research questions posed. Selecting multiple or single cases is a key element, but a case study can include more than one unit of embedded analysis. For example, a case study may involve study of a single industry and a firm participating in that industry. This type of case study involves two levels of analysis and increases the complexity and amount of data to be gathered and analyzed.

A key strength of the case study method involves using multiple sources and techniques in the data gathering process. The researcher determines in advance what evidence to gather and what analysis techniques to use with the data to answer the research questions. Data gathered is normally largely qualitative, but it may also be quantitative. Tools to collect data can include surveys, interviews, documentation review, observation, and even the collection of physical artifacts.

The researcher must use the designated data gathering tools systematically and properly in collecting the evidence. Throughout the design phase, researchers must ensure that the study is well constructed to ensure construct validity, internal validity, external validity, and reliability. Construct validity requires the researcher to use the correct measures for the concepts being studied. Internal validity (especially important with explanatory or causal studies) demonstrates that certain conditions lead to other conditions and requires the use of multiple pieces of evidence from multiple sources to uncover convergent lines of inquiry. The researcher strives to establish a chain of evidence forward and backward. External validity reflects whether or not findings are generalizable beyond the immediate case or cases; the more variations in places, people, and procedures a case study can withstand and still yield the same findings, the more external validity. Techniques such as cross-case examination and within-case examination along with literature review help ensure external validity. Reliability refers to the stability, accuracy, and precision of measurement. Exemplary case study design ensures that the procedures used are well documented and can be repeated with the same results over and over again.

Step 3. Prepare to Collect the Data

Because case study research generates a large amount of data from multiple sources, systematic organization of the data is important to prevent the researcher from becoming overwhelmed by the amount of data and to prevent the researcher from losing sight of the original research purpose and questions. Advance preparation assists in handling large amounts of data in a documented and systematic fashion. Researchers prepare databases to assist with categorizing, sorting, storing, and retrieving data for analysis.

Exemplary case studies prepare good training programs for investigators, establish clear protocols and procedures in advance of investigator field work, and conduct a pilot study in advance of moving into the field in order to remove obvious barriers and problems. The investigator training program covers the basic concepts of the study, terminology, processes, and methods, and teaches investigators how to properly apply the techniques being used in the study. The program also trains investigators to understand how the gathering of data using multiple techniques strengthens the study by providing opportunities for triangulation during the analysis phase of the study. The program covers protocols for case study research, including time deadlines, formats for narrative reporting and field notes, guidelines for collection of documents, and guidelines for field procedures to be used.

Investigators need to be good listeners who can hear exactly the words being used by those interviewed. Qualifications for investigators also include being able to ask good questions and interpret answers. Good investigators review documents looking for facts, but also read between the lines and pursue collaborative evidence elsewhere when that seems appropriate. Investigators need to be flexible in real-life situations and not feel threatened by unexpected change, missed appointments, or lack of office space. Investigators need to understand the purpose of the study and grasp the issues and must be open to contrary findings. Investigators must also be aware that they are going into the world of real human beings who may be threatened or unsure of what the case study will bring.

After investigators are trained, the final advance preparation step is to select a pilot site and conduct a pilot test using each data gathering method so that problematic areas can be uncovered and corrected. Researchers need to anticipate key problems and events, identify key people, prepare letters of introduction, establish rules for confidentiality, and actively seek opportunities to revisit and revise the research design in order to address and add to the original set of research questions.

Step 4. Collect Data in the Field

The researcher must collect and store multiple sources of evidence comprehensively and systematically, in formats that can be referenced and sorted so that converging lines of inquiry and patterns can be uncovered. Researchers carefully observe the object of the case study and identify causal factors associated with the observed phenomenon. Renegotiation of arrangements with the objects of the study or addition of questions to interviews may be necessary as the study progresses. Case study research is flexible, but when changes are made, they are documented systematically.

Exemplary case studies use field notes and databases to categorize and reference data so that it is readily available for subsequent reinterpretation. Field notes record feelings and intuitive hunches, pose questions, and document the work in progress. They record testimonies, stories, and illustrations which can be used in later reports. They may warn of impending bias because of the detailed exposure of the client to special attention, or give an early signal that a pattern is emerging. They assist in determining whether or not the inquiry needs to be reformulated or redefined based on what is being observed. Field notes should be kept separate from the data being collected and stored for analysis.

Maintaining the relationship between the issue and the evidence is mandatory. The researcher may enter some data into a database and physically store other data, but the researcher documents, classifies, and cross-references all evidence so that it can be efficiently recalled for sorting and examination over the course of the study.

Step 5. Evaluate and Analyze the Data

The researcher examines raw data using many interpretations in order to find linkages between the research object and the outcomes with reference to the original research questions. Throughout the evaluation and analysis process, the researcher remains open to new opportunities and insights. The case study method, with its use of multiple data collection methods and analysis techniques, provides researchers with opportunities to triangulate data in order to strengthen the research findings and conclusions.

The tactics used in analysis force researchers to move beyond initial impressions to improve the likelihood of accurate and reliable findings. Exemplary case studies will deliberately sort the data in many different ways to expose or create new insights and will deliberately look for conflicting data to disconfirm the analysis. Researchers categorize, tabulate, and recombine data to address the initial propositions or purpose of the study, and conduct cross-checks of facts and discrepancies in accounts. Focused, short, repeat interviews may be necessary to

20

gather additional data to verify key observations or check a fact.

Specific techniques include placing information into arrays, creating matrices of categories, creating flow charts or other displays, and tabulating frequency of events. Researchers use the quantitative data that has been collected to corroborate and support the qualitative data which is most useful for understanding the rationale or theory underlying relationships. Another technique is to use multiple investigators to gain the advantage provided when a variety of perspectives and insights examine the data and the patterns. When the multiple observations converge, confidence in the findings increases. Conflicting perceptions, on the other hand, cause the researchers to pry more deeply.

Another technique, the cross-case search for patterns, keeps investigators from reaching premature conclusions by requiring that investigators look at the data in many different ways. Cross-case analysis divides the data by type across all cases investigated. One researcher then examines the data of that type thoroughly. When a pattern from one data type is corroborated by the evidence from another, the finding is stronger. When evidence conflicts, deeper probing of the differences is necessary to identify the cause or source of conflict. In all cases, the researcher treats the evidence fairly to produce analytic conclusions answering the original "how" and "why" research questions.

Step 6. Prepare the report

Exemplary case studies report the data in a way that transforms a complex issue into one that can be understood, allowing the reader to question and examine the study and reach an understanding independent of the researcher. The goal of the written report is to portray a complex problem in a way that conveys a vicarious experience to the reader. Case studies present data in very publicly accessible ways and may lead the reader to apply the experience in his or her own real-life situation. Researchers pay particular attention to displaying sufficient evidence to gain the reader's confidence that all avenues have been explored, clearly communicating the boundaries of the case, and giving special attention to conflicting propositions.

Techniques for composing the report can include handling each case as a separate chapter or treating the case as a chronological recounting. Some researchers report the case study as a story. During the report preparation process, researchers critically examine the document looking for ways the report is incomplete. The researcher uses representative audience groups to review and comment on the draft document. Based on the comments, the researcher rewrites and makes revisions. Some case study researchers suggest that the document review audience include a journalist and some suggest that the documents should be reviewed by the participants in the study.

5. Descriptive Research Designs

A descriptive study is one in which information is collected without changing the environment (i.e., nothing is manipulated). Sometimes these are referred to as "correlational" or "observational" studies. Descriptive research design is a type of research method that is used when one wants to get information on the current status of a person or an object. It is used to describe what is in existence in respect to conditions or variables that are found in a given situation

A descriptive study can provide information about the naturally occurring health status, behavior, attitudes or other characteristics of a particular group. Descriptive studies are also conducted to demonstrate associations or relationships between things in the world.

Descriptive studies can involve a one-time interaction with groups of people (cross-sectional study) or a study might follow individuals over time (longitudinal study). Under this study, the researcher interacts with the participant, may involve surveys or interviews to collect the necessary information. Descriptive studies in which the researcher does not interact with the participant include observational studies of people in an environment and studies involving data collection using existing records (e.g. medical record review).

Descriptive research is very common in business and other aspects of life.

Descriptive research can be either quantitative or qualitative. It can involve collections of quantitative information that can be tabulated along a continuum in numerical form, such as scores on a test or describe the categories of information such as gender or patterns of interaction when using technology in a group situation. Descriptive research involves gathering data that describe events and then organizes, tabulates, depicts, and describes the data collection. It often uses visual aids such as graphs and charts to help the reader in understanding the data distribution. Because the human mind cannot extract the full import of a large mass of raw data, descriptive statistics are very important in reducing the data to manageable form. When in-depth, narrative descriptions of small numbers of cases are involved, the research uses description as a tool to organize data into patterns that emerge during analysis. Those patterns aid the mind in comprehending a qualitative study and its implications.

Descriptive studies report summary data such as measures of central tendency including the mean, median, mode, deviance from the mean, variation, percentage, and correlation between variables. Survey research commonly includes that type of measurement, but often goes beyond the descriptive statistics in order to draw inferences. Descriptions of phenomena can also emerge from qualitative studies, case studies, observational studies, interviews, and portfolio assessments.

5.1. Types of Descriptive Research Design

There are two main types of descriptive methods, they are cross sectional and longitudinal. Cross-sectional study involves drawing a sample of elements from the population of interest. Characteristics of the elements, or sample members, are measured only once. But the longitudinal study, the measurement goes repeatedly over time.

5.1. 1. Longitudinal study

A longitudinal study refers to an investigation where participant outcomes and possibly treatments or exposures are collected at multiple follow-up times.

A longitudinal study is a correlational research study that involves repeated observations of the same variables over long periods of time - often many decades. It is a type of observational study.

Longitudinal studies are often used in psychology to study developmental trends across the life span, and in sociology to study life events throughout lifetimes or generations. The reason for this is that unlike cross-sectional studies, in which different individuals with same characteristics are compared, longitudinal studies track the same people, and therefore the differences observed in those people are less likely to be the result of cultural differences across generations.

Longitudinal studies make observing changes more accurate, and they are applied in various other fields. In medicine, the design is used to uncover predictors of certain diseases. In advertising, the design is used to identify the changes that advertising has produced in the attitudes and behaviors of those within the target audience who have seen the advertising campaign.

5.1.1.1. Benefits of longitudinal studies

Longitudinal studies play a key role in epidemiology, clinical research, and therapeutic evaluation. Longitudinal studies are used to characterize normal growth and aging, to assess the effect of risk factors on human health, and to evaluate the effectiveness of treatments. It involve a great deal of effort but offer several benefits. These benefits include:

There are several advantages associated with the longitudinal research design.

• It allows researchers to assess the stability and continuity of several attributes of a sample by repeatedly observing the same participants

• Prospective ascertainment of exposure. In a prospective study participants can have their exposure status recorded at multiple follow-up visits. This can alleviate recall bias where subjects who subsequently experience disease are more likely to recall their exposure (a form of measurement error). In addition the temporal order of exposures and outcomes is observed.

• This type of design also allows researchers to identify developmental trends by looking for common attributes that the subjects share, for example, points at which most children undergo changes

• It avoids cohort effects because the researcher examines one group of people over time, rather than comparing several different groups that represent different ages and generations.

• Measurement of individual change in outcomes. A key strength of a longitudinal study is the ability to measure change in outcomes and/or exposure at the individual level. Longitudinal studies provide the opportunity to observe individual patterns of change.

• This type of design combines both qualitative and quantitative data, creating more in-depth research

5.1.1.2. Challenges of longitudinal studies

The benefits of a longitudinal design are not without cost. There are several challenges posed

• Participant follow-up. There is the risk of bias due to incomplete follow-up, or "drop-out" of study participants. If subjects that are followed to the planned end of study differ from subjects who discontinue follow-up then a naive analysis may provide summaries that are not representative of the original target population.

• The longitudinal research design is subject to high dropout rates of participants, which may also weaken the internal validity of such studies.

• Analysis of correlated data. Statistical analysis of longitudinal data requires methods that can properly account for the intra-subject correlation of response measurements. If such correlation is ignored then inferences such as statistical tests or confidence intervals can be grossly invalid.

• Longitudinal research is very time consuming, for everyone involved. The participants must be highly committed in order to continue and complete the duration of the study, and the researcher must remain interested in the research whilst they wait for years to see the final results.

• Time-varying covariates. Although longitudinal designs offer the opportunity to associate changes in exposure with changes in the outcome of interest, the direction of causality can be complicated by "feedback" between the outcome and the exposure.

• This form of research is also very expensive to conduct, since the researchers must track people down and persuade them to come back and participate in the study. Besides there is added expense of repeatedly training experimenters to conduct the study if it is going to span over many years.

• Practice effects may threaten the validity of a study: participants who are repeatedly tested and interviewed may become increasingly familiar with contents. As a result, they may display performance improvements that are unrelated to the normal patterns of development.

• Since longitudinal studies may go on for a number of years, participants may lose interest in the study, move away or die. When participants drop out of a study, it is known as participant attrition, which can result in smaller and non-representative samples.

The longitudinal developmental research design, the same group of participants are observed and measured at different intervals over a period of time, thus cohort effects are not a problem. Stability, continuity and normative trends can easily be identified and quantitative methods are combined with qualitative methods. Longitudinal studies are very time consuming for both researchers and participants, as well as being extremely expensive. The validity of such studies can be questioned due to practice effects, and participant attrition may create biased and non-representative samples.

5.1.2. Cross-sectional Study

Cross-sectional studies are carried out at one time point or over a short period. They are usually conducted to estimate the prevalence of the outcome of interest for a given population, commonly for the purposes of public health planning. Data can also be collected on individual characteristics, including exposure to risk factors, alongside information about the outcome. In this way cross-sectional studies provide a 'snapshot' of the outcome and the characteristics associated with it, at a specific point in time.

A cross-sectional design is used when the purpose of the study is descriptive, often in the form of a survey. Usually there is no hypothesis as such, but the aim is to describe a population or a subgroup within the population with respect to an outcome and a set of risk factors. It is also used to find the prevalence of the outcome of interest, for the population or subgroups within the population at a given time point.

5.1. 2.1. Benefits of cross-sectional study

• Relatively quick and easy to conduct: It is very easy to conduct a cross sectional research as the data would be collected only once and no need for any follow up action. The duration of the data collection would be 2 to 6 months.
• Data on all variables is only collected once: The researcher collects the data only once in during the study. After reviewing literatures, the researcher interested to empirically check whether the hypothesized relation exists in the population at once.
• Able to measure prevalence for all factors under investigation: It can measure all factors under investigation. The researcher may select factors as per some historical support and focus only such factors to identify any significant changes happened at specific time.

• Multiple outcomes and exposures can be studied: As the duration of the data collection is comparatively short, the researcher can study all possible relations between variables easily.

• Good for descriptive analyses and for generating hypotheses: The cross sectional research gives the state of affairs of a particular distribution through descriptive analysis. It can also used to develop hypothesis for a longer duration research.

5.1. 2.2. Challenges of cross-sectional designs

Cross-sectional studies provide a snapshot of the frequency of certain characteristics in a population at a given point in time.

• Data Gathering and Assessment: The nature of cross-sectional studies offers a quick and easy way for an epidemiologist or any kind of researcher to quickly amass data. While some special case studies do require more specific data, for most cross-sectional studies, routinely collected data will suffice. This allows for quick and easy data gathering even for a large target population. Assessment of outcomes and risk factors for the entire population is also done with little trouble, as the sample is a near-perfect snapshot of the whole.

• Moderate Cost: The ease of gathering the needed information translates to cost-effectiveness. Many hospitals and census bureaus have that information already in hand, saving the researcher the trouble of gathering it, a time-consuming and expensive activity. The low cost involved in cross-sectional studies make it possible to conduct more thorough investigations of the population's overall condition.

• Representative sample: A cross-sectional study should be representative of whole the population, if generalisations from the findings are to have any validity. For example a study of the prevalence of diabetes among women aged 40-60 years in Town A should comprise a random sample of all women aged 40-60 years in that town. If the study is to be representative, attempts should be made to include hard to reach groups, such as people in institutions or the homeless

• Causality: The snapshot nature of cross-sectional studies, while convenient, does have its downside in that it doesn't provide a good basis for establishing causality.

Two distinct variables are measured at the same point in time. Cross-sectional studies can say that the two are related somehow, but they cannot positively determine if one caused the other. Cross-sectional studies also fail on the part of confounding factors. Additional variables may affect the relationship between the variables of interest but not affect those variables themselves. Such observations are often lost in cross-sectional studies.

• Sample size: The sample size should be sufficiently large enough to estimate the prevalence of the conditions of interest with adequate precision. Sample size calculations can be carried out using sample size tables or statistical packages. The larger the study, the less likely the results are due to chance alone, but this will also have implications for cost.

• Data collection: As data on exposures and outcomes are collected simultaneously, specific inclusion and exclusion criteria should be established at the design stage, to ensure that those with the outcome are correctly identified. The data collection methods will depend on the exposure, outcome and study setting, but include questionnaires and interviews, as well as medical examinations. Routine data sources may also be used.

Cross-sectional studies are observational in nature and are known as descriptive research, not causal or relational. Researchers record the information that is present in a population, but they do not manipulate variables. This type of research can be used to describe characteristics that exist in a population, but not to determine cause-and-effect relationships between different variables. These methods are often used to make inferences about possible relationships or to gather preliminary data to support further research and experimentation. Cross sectional research differs from longitudinal research in that cross-sectional studies are designed to look at a variable at a particular point in time. Longitudinal studies involve taking multiple measures over an extended period of time, while cross-sectional research is focused on looking at variables at a specific point in time.

5.1.3. Causal Research Designs

Causality studies may be thought of as understanding a phenomenon in terms of conditional statements in the form, "If X, then Y." This type of research is used to measure what impact a specific change will have on existing norms and assumptions. Most social scientists seek causal explanations that reflect tests of hypotheses. Causal effect occurs when variation in one phenomenon, an independent variable, leads to or results, on average, in variation in another phenomenon, the dependent variable. Identifying causes, figuring out why things happen, is the goal of most social science research. Unfortunately, valid explanations of the causes of social phenomena do not come easily.

A cause is an explanation for some characteristic, attitude, or behavior of groups, individuals, or other entities (such as families, organizations, or cities) or for events. Most social scientists seek causal explanations that reflect tests of the types of hypotheses with which you are familiar. The independent variable is the presumed cause, and the dependent variable is the potential effect. Everyone is familiar with the general notion of causality, the idea that one thing leads to the occurrence of another. The scientific notion of causality is quite complex, however; scientists tell us that it is impossible to prove that one thing causes another.

5.1.3.1. Nomothetic Causal Explanation

A Nomothetic causal explanation exists when there is a correlation between an Independent variable and a dependent variable. That is to say the value of the dependent variable would be different from what it would be if the independent variable occurs or acts upon it. Social Scientists use the nomothetic method when they have an interest that involves social regularities or things that apply to people in general. The data involved in Nomothetic causal explanation is quantitative data, derived from numbers. A nomothetic causal explanation is one involving the belief that variation in an independent variable will be followed by variation in the dependent variable, when all other things are equal (ceteris paribus). In this perspective, researchers who claim a causal effect have concluded that the value of cases on the dependent variable differs from what their value would have been in the absence of variation in the independent variable. For instance, researchers might claim that the likelihood of committing violent crimes is higher for individuals who were abused as children than it would be if these same individuals had not been abused as children. Or, researchers might claim that the likelihood of committing violent crimes is higher for individuals exposed to media violence than it would be if these same individuals had not been exposed to media violence.

5.1.3.2. Idiographic Causal Explanation

An idiographic causal explanation is a scientific explanation that includes a sequence of events that lead to a particular outcome for a specific individual. Stated ideographically, a causal explanation would include initial conditions and then would relate a series of events at different times that led to the outcome. Social Scientists using the Idiographic method are concerned with how a specific result occurs as part of a larger whole or larger set of circumstances that are related. This type of causal explanation is concerned with an understanding of human behavior. This explanation is also more concerned with individual people, places, and events rather than the general population. This concern is also somewhat of a problem. The social researcher can make general conclusions but only based on an indivual, a single place, or a single event. This means that the idiographic method cannot be used to explain any general ideas, places, events, or populations. The information gained is limited to the context of just that specific person, place, and event.

A causal explanation that is idiographic includes statements of initial conditions and then relates a series of events at different times that led to the outcome, or causal effect. This narrative or story is the critical element in an idiographic explanation, which may therefore be classified as narrative reasoning. Idiographic explanations focus on particular social actors, in particular social places, at particular social times. Idiographic explanations are also typically very concerned with context, with understanding the particular outcome as part of a larger set of interrelated circumstances. Idiographic explanations thus can be termed holistic.

Idiographic explanation is deterministic, focusing on what caused a particular event to occur or what caused a particular case to change. As in nomothetic explanations, idiographic causal explanations can involve counterfactuals, by trying to identify what would have happened if a different circumstance had occurred. But unlike in nomothetic explanations, in idiographic explanations the notion of a probabilistic relationship, an average effect, does not really apply. A deterministic cause has an effect in every case under consideration.

5.1.3.3. Criteria for Causal Explanations

When designing research techniques, social scientists use five criteria to decide the accuracy of the results. When research is finished, the researchers need to go back over the data and use the five criteria to help better understand the results. If one of the criteria is not met while conducting research, it becomes difficult to believe the validity of the research. The five criteria are correlation, time order, nonspuriousness, causal mechanism, and context. Correlation, time order, and nonspuriousness are the most important of the criteria, however, causal mechanism and context can also strengthen causal explanations.

• Correlation: It basically establishes that if variation in one variable occurs, then variation in the second variable should follow suit. If values in the independent variable differ in the same terms as the dependent variable, then correlation exists. This test is the same for experimental and non-experimental research. The only difference is that in non-experimental research, the independent variable is not the treatment. To establish a correlation the measurements of the data must be valid, meaning measuring what is supposed to be measured. Validity refers to finding results that correctly show the concept being measured. If a social researcher can ensure a valid measure then the data retrieved is reliable and a correlation is established. If the data found is covering more information than what is necessary it may not show a correlation.

• Time Order: It is also an important criterion for causal explanation. Time order tells us that the variation in the dependent variable did, in fact, occur after variation in the independent variable. Basically, time order says whatever causes the outcome actually has to happen before the outcome. A causes B, but we have to make sure that A actually happened before B. Establishing time order is essential because this will determine the research design and help create causal explanations. Two basic research designs are longitudinal and cross-sectional. The problem that occurs is that a longitudinal research design is the only proper way to establish time order. Longitudinal design occurs at more than one point in time which allows the researcher to ensure that A did indeed occur before B. Due to the fact that cross-sectional design involves gaining data at one point in time it becomes impossible to establish which occurred first, A or B, and therefore making it impossible to establish time order.

• Nonspuriousness: The concept of nonspuriousness draws from the idea of time order. While time order tells us that A absolutely caused B, nonspuriousness tells us something a bit different. In some cases it may be true that A caused B, but maybe a third variable was involved, C, that caused both A and B. In this case A would not have caused B at all. The phrase "correlation does not prove causation" helps us with this concept. This criterion for causation is especially important. It would be easy for an entire set of research to become invalid simply because a third variable was overlooked. A way to deal with nonspuriousness is to consider sampling frame. Sampling frame sets up the boundaries for what will be included in the research. When conducting research, we are able to consider what should be included in our study if it fits into the boundaries that we have set. By setting the boundaries of the sampling frame, a researcher is able to control which causes are studied. Therefore, the researcher can easily check for a nonspurious relationship.

• Causal Mechanism: It is a connection between the variations in the independent and dependent variables that is created by social mechanisms. In a nutshell, a causal mechanism is what causes the relationship between the independent and dependent variables. If there is no connection between the variables, then there is no causal mechanism. Intervening variables help explain the connection between the independent and dependent variables. The intervening variables truly explain the variance between the independent and dependent variables. The only drawback in the intervening variable is that finding it does not guarantee any help in finding the causal mechanism. For any experiment, there can be numerous amounts of causal mechanisms. There is no set number of causal mechanisms in an experiment.

• Context: The context of the data in an experiment needs to deal directly with what the experiment is supposed to be finding. Stemming from context is the contextual effect, which is the reason why something happens differently in different sociological and geographical settings. Identifying the contextual effect can clarify the relationships between the independent and dependent variables. Different types of contextual effect are: race, age, financial status, geography, gender, the list continues on to many other types of contextual effects.

Research design is not related to any particular method of collecting data or any particular type of data. Any research design can, in principle, use any type of data collection method and cause either quantitative or qualitative data. Research design refers to the structure of an enquiry, it is a logical matter rather than a logistical one. It has been argued that the central of research design is to minimize the chance of drawing incorrect causal inferences from data. Design is a logical task undertaken to ensure that the evidence collected enables us to answer questions or to test theories as unambiguously as possible. When designing research it is essential that we identify the type of evidence required to answer the research question in a convincing way. This means that we must not simply collect evidence that is consistent with a particular theory or explanation. Research needs to be structured in such a way that the evidence also bears on alternative rival explanations and enables us to identify which of the competing explanations is most compelling empirically. It also means that we must not simply look for evidence that supports our favorite theory; we should also look for evidence that has the potential to disprove our preferred explanations.

Suggested Reading

Barbara Geddes. (1990). "How the cases you choose affect the answers you get: Selection Bias in Comparative Politics," in Political Analysis. 2:131-49.

Beiderbeck AB, Sturkenboom MC, Coebergh JW et al. (2004). Misclassification of exposure is high when interview data on drug use are used as a proxy measure of chronic drug use during follow-up. J Clin Epidemiol. 57:973-7.

Bland M.(2001). An Introduction to Medical Statistics. 3rd Edn. Oxford: Oxford University Press.

Bond TG, Fox CM. (2001). Applying the Rasch model: fundamental measurement in the human sciences. Mahwah, NJ: Lawrence Erlbaum, 1-288.

Boog, B., Coenen, H., Keune. L., & Lammerts, R. (Eds.). (1998). The complexity of relationships in action research. Tilburg, The Netherlands: Tilburg University Press.

Boog, Ben, et al. (1996). Theory and Practice of Action Research - With Special Reference to the Netherlands. Tilburg, The Netherlands: Tilbury University Press.

Bovaird, James A. & Kevin A. Kupzyk.(2010). "Sequential Design." In *Encyclopedia of Research*

Design. Neil J. Salkind, ed. Thousand Oaks, CA: Sage..

Boyd, H.W. Jr. and Westfall, R. (1972). Marketing Research: Text and Cases, Irwin, p. 80.

Franklin, Beth. (1998). An accounting of the outcomes has not yet been published. Toronto/York University, 10/2.

Freeley, A. J. (1976). Argumentation and debate: rational decision making. Belmont, CA: Wadsworth.

Frison L.J. and Pocock S.J. (1992). Repeated measures in clinical trials: analysis using summary statistics and its implication for design. Statistics in Medicine, 11: 1685–1704.

Frison L.J. and Pocock S.J. (1997). Linearly divergent treatment effects in clinical trials with repeated measures: efficient analysis using summary statistics. Statistics in Medicine, 16: 2855–2872.

Gall, Meredith. (2007). Educational Research: An Introduction. Chapter 18, Action Research. 8th ed. Boston, MA: Pearson/Allyn and Bacon.

Gall, Meredith. (2007). *Educational Research: An Introduction.* Chapter 11, Nonexperimental Research: Correlational Designs. 8th ed. Boston, MA: Pearson/Allyn and Bacon.

Gall, Meredith. (2007). *Educational Research: An Introduction*. Chapter 16, Historical Research. 8th ed. Boston, MA: Pearson/Allyn and Bacon.

Garraghan, G. J. (1946). A Guide to Historical Method. New York: Fordham University Press.

Geertz, C. (1973). The interpretation of cultures. New York: Basic Books.

Gilbert EH, Lowenstein SR, Koziol-McLain J et al. (1996). Chart reviews in emergency medicine research: where are the methods? Ann Emerg Med. 27: 305-8.

Gilmore, Thomas, Jim Krantz, and Rafael Ramirez. (2000). "Action Based Modes of Inquiry and the Host-Researcher Relationship." Consultation 5.3: 160-76.
Glaser, B. G. & Strauss, A. L. (1967). The discovery of grounded theory: Strategies for qualitative research. Chicago: Aldine.

Goldhor, H. (1972). An introduction to scientific research in librarianship. Urbana, IL: University of Illinois.

Gottschalk, L. (1951). Understanding History. New York : Alfred A. Knopf.

Gottschalk, L. A. (1995). Content analysis of verbal behavior: New findings and clinical applications. Hillside, NJ: Lawrence Erlbaum Associates, Inc

Govier, T. (1985). A practical study of argument. Belmont, CA: Wadsworth.

Green, P.E., Tull, D.S. and Albaum, G. (1993), Research For Marketing Decisions, 5th edition, Prentice-Hall, pp. 105-107

Greenwood, Davydd, William Foote Whyte, and Ira Harkavy. (1993). "Participatory Action Research as a Process and as a Goal." Human Relations 46.2: 175-92.
Grimes DA, Schultz KF. (2002). Cohort studies: marching towards outcomes. Lancet; 359:341–345.

Grosh, Margaret, and Paul Glewwe, eds. (2000). Designing Household Survey Questionnaires for Developing Countries: Lessons from 15 Years of the Living Standards Measurement Study. New York: Oxford University Press (for World Bank).

Guba, E. G., & Lincoln, Y. S. (1989). Fourth generation evaluation. London: Sage.

Hall, Budd L. (1992). "From Margins to Centre? The Development and Purpose of Participatory Research." American Sociologist Winter, 15-28.

Hall, John. (2008). "Cross-Sectional Survey Design." In *Encyclopedia of Survey Research Methods*. Paul J. Lavrakas, ed. (Thousand Oaks, CA: Sage), pp. 173-174;

Hambleton RK, Swaminathan H, Rogers HJ. (1991). Fundamentals of item response theory. Newbury Park, CA: Sage,1-153.

Hamel, J., Dufour, S., & Fortin, D.). (1993). Case study methods. Newbury Park, CA: Sage.

Hanley, J.A., Negassa, A., deB. Edwardes, M.D., and Forrester J.E. (2003). Statistical analysis of correlated data using generalized estimating equations: An orientation. American Journal of Epidemiology, 157: 364–375.

Harkness, Janet A., Fons J.R. Van de Vijver and Peter Mohler (2003). Cross-Cultural Survey Methods. New York: Wiley

Harris, S., & Sutton, R. (1986). Functions of parting ceremonies in dying organizations. Academy of Management Journal, 19, 5-30.

Healy P, Devane D. (2011). "Methodological Considerations in Cohort Study Designs." Nurse Researcher 18, 32-36;

Helen Barratt, Maria Kirwan. (2009). Cross-Sectional Studies: Design, Application, Strengths and Weaknesses of Cross-Sectional Studies. Healthknowledge,

Hennekens CH, Buring JE. (1987). Epidemiology in Medicine, Lippincott Williams & Wilkins.

Heron, J. (1981). Philosophical basis for a new paradigm. In: P. Reason, & J. Rowan (Eds.) Human inquiry:A sourcebook of new paradigm research (pp. 19-36). Chicester, UK: John Wiley.

Hogan, J.W., and Laird, N.M. (1997). Mixture models for the joint distribution of repeated measures and event times. Statistics in Medicine, 16: 239–257.

Hogan, J.W., and Laird, N.M. (1997). Model-based approaches to analyzing incomplete longitudinal and failure time data. Statistics in Medicine, 16:259–272.

Hollingsworth, Sandra (ed.). (1997). International Action Research: A Casebook for Educational Reform. London: The Falmer Press.

Howes, C., & Matheson, C. C. (1992). Sequences in the development of competent play with peers: Social and social pretend play. *Developmental Psychology*, 28, 961-974.

http://allpsych.com/researchmethods/validityreliability.html

http://campus.udayton.edu/~jrs/tools/notes/exploratory%20research.pdf

http://campus.udayton.edu/~jrs/tools/notes/exploratory%20research.pdf

http://dissertation.laerd.com/probability-sampling.php

http://dissertation.laerd.com/probability-sampling.php

http://en.wikipedia.org/wiki/Dialectic

http://en.wikipedia.org/wiki/Logical_argument

http://en.wikipedia.org/wiki/Methodic_Doubt

http://en.wikipedia.org/wiki/Methodic_Doubt

http://en.wikipedia.org/wiki/Philosophical_method

http://guides.is.uwa.edu.au/content.php?pid=43218&sid=318559

http://guides.mclibrary.duke.edu/content.php?pid=431451&sid=3530451

http://johngarger.com/articles/methodology/4-levels of measurement in social science research

http://korbedpsych.com/R06Sample.html

http://libguides.usc.edu/content.php?pid=83009&sid=818072

http://libguides.usc.edu/content.php?pid=83009&sid=818072

http://libguides.usc.edu/content.php?pid=83009&sid=818072

http://lynn-library.libguides.com/researchmethodsd8

http://psych.csufresno.edu/psy144/Content/Design/N
onexperimental/observation.html on 18th April 2014

http://sphweb.bumc.bu.edu/ on 17th March 2014

http://top-copywriter.com/essential-elements-of-a-
case-study/ on 12th December 2013

http://universalteacher.com/1/disadvantages-of-
exploratory-research/

Miles, M. B., & Huberman, A. M. (1984).
Qualitative data analysis: A sourcebook of new
methods. Beverly Hills, CA: Sage.

Miller L. E., & Smith, K. (1983). Handling non-
response issues. Journal of Extension On-line, 21(5).
Available at: http://www.joe.org/joe/1983september/
83-5-a7.pdf

Miller, F. (1986). Use, appraisal, and research: A
case study of social history. The American Archivist:
49(4), 371-392.

Mitchell, J. C. (1983). Case and situational analysis.
The Sociological Review, 31(2), 187-211.

Natalie Davis. (1987). Fiction in the Archives:
Pardon Tales and their Tellers in Sixteenth-Century
France, Stanford University Press, 1987.

Nataliya V. Ivankova. (2008). Using Mixed-Methods
Sequential Explanatory Design: From Theory to
Practice.

Neville, C. (2007). The complete guide to referencing and avoiding plagiarism. New York: Open University Press.

Nowak, R. (1994). Problems in clinical trials go far beyond misconduct. Science.

Nunnally JC, Bernstein IH.(1994). Psychometric theory. 3rd ed. New York: McGraw-Hill.

Paris, M. (1988). Library school closings: Four case studies. Metuchen, NJ: Scarecrow Press.

Patton, M (1990) Qualitative evaluation and research methods, Sage Publications, Newbury Park, California.

Patton, M. Q. (1980). Qualitative evaluation methods. Beverly Hills, CA: Sage.

Patton, M. Q. (1986). Utilization-focused evaluation. London: Sage.

Patton, M. Q. (1990). Qualitative evaluation and research methods. London: Sage.

Pelham, B. W.; Blanton, H. (2006). *Conducting Research in Psychology: Measuring the Weight of Smoke, 3rd Edition.* Wadsworth Publishing.

Peter Evans, Contribution to "The Role of Theory in Comparative Politics: A Symposium," World Politics 48, n11 (October 1995).

Ployhart, Robert E. and Robert J. Vandenberg. (2010). "Longitudinal Research: The Theory, Design, and Analysis of Change." *Journal of Management*: 94-120

Ployhart, Robert E. and Robert J. Vandenberg. (2010). "Longitudinal Research: The Theory, Design, and Analysis of Change." *Journal of Management*: 94-120

Porta, Miquel, ed. (2008). A Dictionary of Epidemiology (5th ed.). New York: Oxford University Press.

Porta, Miquel, ed. (2008). A Dictionary of Epidemiology (5th ed.). New York: Oxford University Press.

Powell, R. R. (1985). Basic research methods for librarians. Norwood, NJ: Ablex.

Powell, R. R. (1985). Basic research methods for librarians. Norwood, NJ: Ablex.

Power C and Elliott J (2006). "Cohort profile: 1958 British Cohort Study". International Journal of Epidemiology 35 (1): 34–41.

Power C and Elliott J (2006). "Cohort profile: 1958 British Cohort Study". International Journal of Epidemiology 35 (1): 34–41.

Preisser, J.S., Lohman, K.K., and Rathouz, P.J. (2002). Performance of weighted estimating equations for longitudinal binary data with dropouts missing at random. Statistics in Medicine, 21: 3035–3054.

Preisser, J.S., Lohman, K.K., and Rathouz, P.J. (2002). Performance of weighted estimating equations for longitudinal binary data with dropouts missing at random. Statistics in Medicine, 21: 3035–3054.

Reason, P. (Ed.). (1994). Participation in human inquiry. London: Sage.

Reason, P. (Ed.). (1994). Participation in human inquiry. London: Sage.

Reason, Peter and Hilary Bradbury. (2001). Handbook of Action Research: Participative Inquiry and Practice. Thousand Oaks, CA: SAGE.

Reason, Peter and Hilary Bradbury. (2001). Handbook of Action Research: Participative Inquiry and Practice. Thousand Oaks, CA: SAGE.

Rescher, N. (1964). Introduction to logic. New York: St. Martin's Press.

Rescher, N. (1964). Introduction to logic. New York: St. Martin's Press.

Resnik, D. (2000). Statistics, ethics, and research: an agenda for educations and reform. Accountability in Research. 8: 163-88

Robins J.M. (1986). A new approach to causal inference in mortality studies with sustained exposure periods - application to control of the healthy worker survivor effect. Mathematical Modelling.

Robins J.M., Greenland S., and Hu F.-C. (1999). Estimation of the causal effect of a time-varying exposure on the marginal mean of a repeated binary outcome (with discussion). Journal of the American Statistical Association. pp 687–712.

Robins J.M., Rotnitzky A., and Zhao L.P. (1995). Analysis of semi-parametric regression models for repeated outcomes in the presence of missing data. Journal of the American Statistical Association, pp 106–121.

Rosenbaum, Paul R. (2010). *Design of Observational Studies*. New York: Springer.

Samet J.M., Dominici F., Curriero F.C., Coursac I. and Zeger S.L. (2000). Fine particulate air pollution and mortality in 20 US cities. New England Journal of Medicine, 343(24): 1798–1799.

Savitt, Ronald.(1980). Historical Research in Marketing. *Journal of Marketing* pp 52-58.

Schafer J.L. (1997). Analysis of Incomplete Multivariate Data. Chapman and Hall, New York, NY.

Schindler, D. (1996). Urban youth and the frail elderly: Reciprocal giving and receiving. New York: Garland.

Schwarz N, Oyserman D. (2001). Asking questions about behavior: cognition, communication and questionnaire construction. Am J Eval. Pp 127-60.

Schwarz N. (1999). Self-reports: how the questions shape the answers. Am Psychol. Vol. 54: pp93-105.

Seale, C. (1999). The quality of qualitative research. London: Sage.

Shafer, R. J. (1974). A Guide to Historical Method. Illinois : The Dorsey Press..

Shamoo, A.E. (1989). Principles of Research Data Audit. Gordon and Breach, New York.

Shamoo, A.E., Resnik, B.R. (2003). Responsible Conduct of Research. Oxford University Press.

Shepard, R.J. (2002). Ethics in exercise science research. Sports Med, 32 (3): 169-183.

Smith EV, Smith RM. (2004), Introduction to Rasch measurement. Maple Grove, MN: JAM.

Squires BP, Elmslie TJ. (1990). Cohort studies: what editors want from authors and peer reviewers. CMAJ, Vol. 143:179–180.

Stake, R. E. (1978). The case study method in social inquiry. Educational Researcher ,7(2), 5-8.

Stake, R. E. (1995). The art of case study research. Thousand Oaks, CA: Sage.

Stake, R. E. (Ed.). (1975). Evaluating the arts in education: A responsive approach. Colombus, OH: Merrill.

Stanford Encyclopedia of Philosophy. Metaphysics Research Lab, CSLI, Stanford University, 2013.

Stram D.O. and Lee J.W. (1994). Variance component testing in the longitudinal mixed model. Biometrics, 50: 1171–1177.

Strauss, A. L. & Corbin, J. (1990). Basics of qualitative research: Grounded theory, procedures and techniques. London: Sage.

Sudman S, Bradburn N, Schwarz N. (1996). Thinking about answers: the application of cognitive processes to survey methodology. San Francisco: Jossey-Bass.

Sudman, S. and Bradburn, N. M. (1973), Asking Questions, pp. 208 - 28.

Swisher, R., & McClure, C. R. (1984). Research for decision making, methods for librarians. Chicago: American Library Association.

Taylor, P. J., G. Catalano, and D.R.F. Walker. (2002). "Exploratory Analysis of the World City Network." *Urban Studies*.

Taylor, R. S. (1967). Question-negotiation and information-seeking in libraries. Bethlehem, PA: Center for the Information Sciences.

Thomas Ferguson. (1995). Golden Rule: The Investment Theory of Party Competition and the Logic of Money-Driven Political System. University of Chicago Press.

Thomas Gilmore, Jim Krantz and Rafael Ramirez. (1986). Action Based Modes of Inquiry and the Host-Researcher Relationship.

Thompson, B., Noferi, G. (2002). Statistical, practical, clinical: How many types of significance should be considered in counseling research? Journal of Counseling & Development, 80(4):64-71.

Tooth L, Ware R, Bain C, Purdie DM, Dobson A. (2005). Quality of reporting of observational longitudinal research. Am J Epidemiol; 161:280–288.

Trochim, William M.K. (2006). Experimental Design. Research Methods Knowledge Base.

U.S. Department of Education. (1988). Rethinking the library in the information age: Issues in library research: proposals for the 1990s. Volume II. Washington, DC.

Verbeke G. and Molenberghs G. (2000). Linear Mixed Models for Longitudinal Data. Springer-Verlag, New York, NY.

Walker, J. R., & Taylor, T. (2006). The Columbia guide to online style (2nd ed.). Chichester, West Sussex: Columbia University Press.

Walton, D. N. (1989). Informal logic. A handbook for critical argumentation. Cambridge, MA: Cambridge University Press.

Watkins C, Daniels L, Jack C et al. (2001). Accuracy of a single question in screening for depression in a cohort of patients after stroke: comparative study. BMJ. 17:1159.

Wei, L.J., Lin, D., and Weissfeld, L. (1989). Regression analysis of multivariate incomplete failure time data by modeling marginal distributions. Journal of the American Statistical Association, 84: 1065–1073.

Weiss S.T. and Ware J.H. (1996). Overview of issues in the longitudinal analysis of respiratory data. American Journal of Respiratory Critical Care Medicine, 154: S208–S211.

Weiss, C.H., & Bucuvala, M. J. (1980). Social science research and decision-making. New York: Columbia University Press.

Wester, F. (1995). Strategieën voor kwalitatief onderzoek. Bussum, The Netherlands: Coutinho.

Wholey, J. S., Hatry, H. P., & Newcomer, K. E. (Eds.). (1994). Handbook of practical program evaluation. San Francisco: Jossey-Bass.

Wiseman, F. (2003). On the reporting of response rates in Extension Research. Journal of Extension On-line 41(3), Available at: http://www.joe.org/joe/2003june/comm1.shtml

Yawn BP, Wollan P. (2005). Interrater reliability: completing the methods description in medical records review studies. Am J Epi-demiol.; 161:974-7.

Yin, R. K. (1984). Case study research: Design and methods. Newbury Park, CA: Sage.

Yin, R.K. (1984) Case study research: Design and methods. London: Sage.

****

14979270R00041

Printed in Great Britain
by Amazon.co.uk, Ltd.,
Marston Gate.